ONE HUNDRED AND ONE POEMS OF ROMANCE

CB
CONTEMPORARY
BOOKS
CHICAGO

Library of Congress Cataloging-in-Publication Data

One hundred and one poems of romance / [compiled by Christine Benton].
      p.   cm.
    ISBN 0-8092-3929-9 (cloth)
     1. Love poetry.   I. Benton, Christine.
PN6110.L6049   1992
808.81'9354—dc20   92-15046
                                    CIP

This anthology was compiled by Christine M. Benton.

Published by Contemporary Books, Inc.
180 North Michigan Avenue, Chicago, Illinois 60601
Manufactured in the United States of America
International Standard Book Number: 0-8092-3929-9

PREFACE

The lovers' tradition of communicating through poetry is as old as courtship itself. Today as much as in the distant past, finely wrought verse has the power to vanquish the unconquerable heart and to state profound truths about the nature of love. In just a few words a poem can express what volumes of prose cannot.

In this book are poems that speak of romance in its many forms. Each, in its own way, is a love letter—some paeans, some promises, some pleas—and as such is meant to be shared between lover and beloved. The poets convey the wealth of feelings connected with love: the unrivaled joy of a new romance, the bleak despair of "love without hope," the poignant "ache of marriage," the deep beauty of the "dailiness of life." Here are persuasive arguments for "plucking the fruit"—love as the link between the mortal and the divine, as the wellspring of all human dreams.

Some of these poems are classics; many were penned by our best-loved poets. Others are less well known but no less evocative. All are visions of love, from the sentimental to the sublime.

Perhaps there are two reasons that poems of romance touch our souls: First is the awe-inspiring courage of the poet-lover; what beloved could fail to succumb to the desires of one whose "heart keeps open house," whose love as Theodore Roethke proclaims has "no disguise"? But possibly even more compelling is the poet's ability to capture in any tangible medium something as elusive and all-consuming as love. "Poetry should be great and unobtrusive," said John Keats, "a thing which enters into one's soul, and does not startle or amaze with itself, but with its subject." It is that quality that makes the following selections so enduring.

IF YOU WERE COMING
IN THE FALL (511)

EMILY DICKINSON
(1830–1886)

If you were coming in the Fall,
I'd brush the Summer by
With half a smile, and half a spurn,
As Housewives do, a Fly.

If I could see you in a year,
I'd wind the months in balls—
And put them each in separate Drawers,
For fear the numbers fuse—

If only Centuries, delayed,
I'd count them on my Hand,
Subtracting, till my fingers dropped
Into Van Dieman's Land.

If certain, when this life was out—
That your's and mine, should be—
I'd toss it yonder, like a Rind,
And take Eternity—

But, now, uncertain of the length
Of this, that is between,
It goads me, like the Goblin Bee—
That will not state—it's sting.

LONGING

MATTHEW ARNOLD
(1822–1888)

Come to me in my dreams, and then
By day I shall be well again.
For then the night will more than pay
The hopeless longing of the day.

Come, as thou cam'st a thousand times,
A messenger from radiant climes,
And smile on thy new world, and be
As kind to others as to me.

Or, as thou never cam'st in sooth,
Come now, and let me dream it truth.
And part my hair, and kiss my brow,
And say—*My love! why sufferest thou?*

Come to me in my dreams, and then
By day I shall be well again.
For then the night will more than pay
The hopeless longing of the day.

YOUR LETTER DOES NOT MOVE ME

HEINRICH HEINE
(1797–1856)

Your letter does not move me
    Although the words are strong;
You say you will not love me—
    But ah, the letter's long.

Twelve pages, neat and double.
    A little essay! Why,
One never takes such trouble
    To write a mere good-bye.

TRANSLATED BY LOUIS UNTERMEYER

OUT OF SIGHT, OUT OF MIND

BARNABE GOOGE
(1540–1594)

The oftener seen, the more I lust,
   The more I lust, the more I smart,
The more I smart, the more I trust,
   The more I trust, the heavier heart,
The heavy heart breeds mine unrest,
Thy absence, therefore, like I best.

The rarer seen, the less in mind,
   The less in mind, the lesser pain,
The lesser pain, less grief I find,
   The lesser grief, the greater gain,
The greater gain, the merrier I,
Therefore I wish thy sight to fly.

The further off, the more I joy,
   The more I joy, the happier life,
The happier life, less hurts annoy,
   The lesser hurts, pleasure most rife:
Such pleasures rife shall I obtain
When distance doth depart us twain.

WISHES

Judith Wright
(1915–   )

What would I wish to be?
I wish to be wise.
From the swamps of fear and greed
free me and let me rise.
There was a poet once
spoke clear as a well-cast bell.
Rumí his name; his voice
rings perfect still.
O could I make one verse
but half so well!

What do I wish to do?
I wish to love:
that verb at whose source all verbs
take fire and learn to move.
Yes, could I rightly love,
all action, all event,
would from my nature spring
true as creation meant.
Love takes no pains with words
but is most eloquent.

To love, and to be wise?
Down, fool, and lower your eyes.

WILL NOT COME BACK

ROBERT LOWELL
(1917–1977)

Dark swallows will doubtless come back killing
the injudicious nightflies with a clack of the
beak;
but these that stopped full flight to see your
beauty
and my good fortune . . . as if they knew our
names—
they'll not come back. The thick lemony
honeysuckle,
climbing from the earthroot to your window,
will open more beautiful blossoms to the
evening;
but these . . . like dewdrops, trembling,
shining, falling,
the tears of day—they'll not come back. . . .
Some other love will sound his fireword for
you
and wake your heart, perhaps, from its cool
sleep;
but silent, absorbed, and on his knees,
as men adore God at the altar, as I love you—
don't blind yourself, you'll not be loved like
that.

NEVER SEEK TO TELL THY LOVE

WILLIAM BLAKE
(1757–1827)

Never seek to tell thy love,
Love that never told can be;
For the gentle wind does move
Silently, invisibly.

I told my love, I told my love,
I told her all my heart;
Trembling, cold, in ghastly fears,
Oh! she doth depart.

Soon as she was gone from me,
A traveller came by,
Silently, invisibly:
He took her with a sigh.

PLAYBOY

RICHARD WILBUR
(1921–   )

High on his stockroom ladder like a dunce
The stock-boy sits, and studies like a sage
The subject matter of one glossy page,
As lost in curves as Archimedes once.

Sometimes, without a glance, he feeds himself.
The left hand, like a mother-bird in flight,
Brings him a sandwich for a sidelong bite,
And then returns it to a dusty shelf.

What so engrosses him? The wild décor
Of this pink-papered alcove into which
A naked girl has stumbled, with its rich
Welter of pelts and pillows on the floor,

Amidst which, kneeling in a supple pose,
She lifts a goblet in her farther hand,
As if about to toast a flower-stand
Above which hovers an exploding rose

Fired from a long-necked crystal vase that rests
Upon a tasseled and vermilion cloth
One taste of which would shrivel up a moth?
Or is he pondering her perfect breasts?

Nothing escapes him of her body's grace
Or of her floodlit skin, so sleek and warm
And yet so strangely like a uniform,
But what now grips his fancy is her face,

And how the cunning picture holds her still
At just that smiling instant when her soul,
Grown sweetly faint, and swept beyond control,
Consents to his inexorable will.

THIS LIVING HAND

JOHN KEATS
(1795–1821)

This living hand, now warm and capable
Of earnest grasping, would, if it were cold
And in the icy silence of the tomb,
So haunt thy days and chill thy dreaming nights
That thou wouldst wish thine own heart dry of
    blood
So in my veins red life might stream again,
And thou be conscience-calmed—see here it
    is—
I hold it towards you.

NO MORE, MY DEAR . . .

Sir Philip Sidney
(1554–1586)

No more, my dear, no more these counsels try;
  Oh, give my passions leave to run their race;
  Let fortune lay on me her worst disgrace;
  Let folk o'ercharged with brain against me
    cry;
Let clouds bedim my face, break in mine eye;
  Let me no steps but of lost labor trace;
  Let all the earth with scorn recount my case,
  But do not will me from my love to fly.
I do not envy Aristotle's wit,
  Nor do aspire to Cæsar's bleeding fame;
  Nor aught do care though some above me sit;
Nor hope nor wish another course to frame,
  But that which once may win thy cruel
    heart;
  Thou art my wit, and thou my virtue art.

THE ACHE OF MARRIAGE

Denise Levertov
(1923–   )

The ache of marriage:

thigh and tongue, beloved,
are heavy with it,
it throbs in the teeth

We look for communion
and are turned away, beloved,
each and each

It is leviathan and we
in its belly
looking for joy, some joy
not to be known outside it

two by two in the ark of
the ache of it.

ANNIVERSARY

Richmond Lattimore
(1906–1984)

Where were we in that afternoon? And where
is the high room now, the bed on which you
    laid your hair,
as bells beat early in the still air?

At two o'clock of sun and shutters. Oh, recall
the chair's angle a stripe of shadow on the
    wall,
the hours we gathered in our hands, and then
    let fall.

Wrist on wrist we relive memory, shell of
    moon
on day-sky, two o'clock in lazy June,
and twenty years gone in an afternoon.

A SONG OF PRAISE

(For one who praised his lady's being fair.)

COUNTEE CULLEN
(1903–1946)

You have not heard my love's dark throat,
  Slow-fluting like a reed,
Release the perfect golden note
  She caged there for my need.

Her walk is like the replica
  Of some barbaric dance
Wherein the soul of Africa
  Is winged with arrogance.

And yet so light she steps across
  The ways her sure feet pass,
She does not dent the smoothest moss
  Or bend the thinnest grass.

My love is dark as yours is fair,
  Yet lovelier I hold her
Than listless maids with pallid hair,
  And blood that's thin and colder.

You-proud-and-to-be-pitied one,
  Gaze on her and despair;
Then seal your lips until the sun
  Discovers one as fair.

FIRST LOVE

JOHN CLARE
(1793–1864)

I ne'er was struck before that hour
   With love so sudden and so sweet,
Her face it bloomed like a sweet flower
   And stole my heart away complete.
My face turned pale as deadly pale.
   My legs refused to walk away,
And when she looked, what could I ail?
   My life and all seemed turned to clay.

And then my blood rushed to my face
   And took my eyesight quite away,
The trees and bushes round the place
   Seemed midnight at noonday.
I could not see a single thing,
   Words from my eyes did start—
They spoke as chords do from the string,
   And blood burnt round my heart.

Are flowers the winter's choice?
   Is love's bed always snow?
She seemed to hear my silent voice,
   Not love's appeals to know.
I never saw so sweet a face
   As that I stood before.
My heart has left its dwelling-place
   And can return no more.

KIND AND TRUE

Aurelian Townshend
(1583–1643)

'Tis not how witty nor how free,
Nor yet how beautiful she be,
But how much kind and true to me.
Freedom and wit none can confine
And beauty like the sun doth shine,
But kind and true are only mine.

Let others with attention sit
To listen, and admire her wit,
That is a rock where I'll not split.
Let others dote upon her eyes
And burn their hearts for sacrifice,
Beauty's a calm where danger lies.

But kind and true have been long tried
A harbour where we may confide,
And safely there at anchor ride.
From change of winds there we are free
And need not fear storms' tyranny,
Nor pirate though a prince he be.

SONNET 130

WILLIAM SHAKESPEARE
(1564–1616)

My mistress' eyes are nothing like the sun;
Coral is far more red than her lips' red:
If snow be white, why then her breasts are
    dun;
If hairs be wires, black wires grow on her
    head.
I have seen roses damask'd, red and white,
But no such roses see I in her cheeks;
And in some perfumes is there more delight
Than in the breath that from my mistress reeks.
I love to hear her speak, yet well I know
That music hath a far more pleasing sound:
I grant I never saw a goddess go,—
My mistress, when she walks, treads on the
    ground:
   And yet, by heaven, I think my love as rare
   As any she belied with false compare.

my sweet old etcetera

e. e. cummings
(1894–1962)

my sweet old etcetera
aunt lucy during the recent

war could and what
is more did tell you just
what everybody was fighting

for,
my sister
isabel created hundreds
(and
hundreds)of socks not to

mention shirts fleaproof earwarmers
etcetera wristers etcetera, my
mother hoped that

i would die etcetera
bravely of course my father used
to become hoarse talking about how it was
a privilege and if only he
could meanwhile my

self etcetera lay quietly
in the deep mud et

cetera
(dreaming,
et
    cetera, of
Your smile
eyes knees and of your Etcetera)

WHAT IS SO RARE
AS A DAY IN JUNE?

JAMES RUSSELL LOWELL
(1819–1891)

No price is set on the lavish summer,
And June may be had by the poorest comer.
And what is so rare as a day in June?
   Then, if ever, come perfect days;
Then Heaven tries the earth if it be in tune,
   And over it softly her warm ear lays:
Whether we look, or whether we listen,
We hear life murmur, or see it glisten;
Every clod feels a stir of might,
   An instinct within it that reaches and towers
And, groping blindly above it for light,
   Climbs to a soul in grass and flowers;
The flush of life may well be seen
   Thrilling back over hills and valleys;
The cowslip startles in meadows green,
   The buttercup catches the sun in its chalice
And there's never a leaf or a blade too mean
   To be some happy creature's palace;
The little bird sits at his door in the sun,
   Atilt like a blossom among the leaves,
And lets his illumined being o'errun
   With the deluge of summer it receives;
His mate feels the eggs beneath her wings,
And the heart in her dumb breast flutters and
     sings;
He sings to the wide world, and she to her
     nest,—

In the nice ear of Nature, which song is the
    best?

Now is the high-tide of the year,
    And whatever of life hath ebbed away
Comes flooding back, with a ripply cheer,
    Into every bare inlet and creek and bay;
Now the heart is so full that a drop overfills it,
We are happy now because God wills it;
No matter how barren the past may have been,
'Tis enough for us now that the leaves are
    green;
We sit in the warm shade and feel right well
How the sap creeps up and the blossoms swell;
We may shut our eyes, but we cannot help
    knowing
That skies are clear and grass is growing;
That breeze comes whispering in our ear,
That dandelions are blossoming near,
    That maize has sprouted, that streams are
    flowing,
That the river is bluer than the sky,
That the robin is plastering his house hard by;
And if the breeze kept the good news back,
For other couriers we should not lack;
    We could guess it all by yon heifer's
    lowing,—
And hark! how clear bold chanticleer,
Warmed with the new wine of the year,
    Tells all in his lusty crowing!

Joy comes, grief goes, we know not how;
Everything is happy now,
    Everything is upward striving;
'Tis as easy now for the heart to be true
As for grass to be green or skies to be blue,—
    'Tis the natural way of living:
Who knows whither the clouds have fled?
    In the unscarred heaven they leave no wake,
And the eyes forget the tears they have shed,
    The heart forgets its sorrow and ache;
The soul partakes the season's youth,
    And the sulphurous rifts of passion and woe
Lie deep 'neath a silence pure and smooth,
    Like burnt-out craters healed with snow.

THE RHODORA:
On Being Asked,
Whence is the Flower?

RALPH WALDO EMERSON
(1803–1882)

In May, when sea-winds pierced our solitudes,
I found the fresh Rhodora in the woods,
Spreading its leafless blooms in a damp nook,
To please the desert and the sluggish brook.
The purple petals, fallen in the pool,
Made the black water with their beauty gay;
Here might the red-bird come his plumes to
    cool,
And court the flower that cheapens his array.
Rhodora! if the sages ask thee why
This charm is wasted on the earth and sky,
Tell them, dear, that if eyes were made for
    seeing,
Then Beauty is its own excuse for being:
Why thou wert there, O rival of the rose!
I never thought to ask, I never knew:
But, in my simple ignorance, suppose
The self-same Power that brought me there
    brought you.

SHANE O'NEILL'S CAIRN

To U.J.

ROBINSON JEFFERS
(1887–1962)

When you and I on the Palos Verdes cliff
Found life more desperate than dear,
And when we hawked at it on the lake by
    Seattle,
In the west of the world, where hardly
Anything has died yet: we'd not have been
    sorry, Una,
But surprised, to foresee this gray
Coast in our days, the gray waters of the
    Moyle
Below us, and under our feet
The heavy black stones of the cairn of the lord
    of Ulster.
A man of blood who died bloodily
Four centuries ago: but death's nothing, and
    life,
From a high death-mark on a headland
Of this dim island of burials, is nothing either.
How beautiful are both these nothings.

HOW DO I LOVE THEE? LET ME COUNT THE WAYS

ELIZABETH BARRETT BROWNING
(1806–1861)

How do I love thee? Let me count the ways.
I love thee to the depth and breadth and height
My soul can reach, when feeling out of sight
For the ends of Being and ideal Grace.
I love thee to the level of everyday's
Most quiet need, by sun and candle-light.
I love thee freely, as men strive for Right;
I love thee purely, as they turn from Praise.
I love thee with the passion put to use
In my old griefs, and with my childhood's
  faith.
I love thee with a love I seemed to lose
With my lost saints,—I love thee with the
  breath,
Smiles, tears, of all my life!—and, if God
  choose,
I shall but love thee better after death.

ECHO

Thomas Moore
(1779–1852)

How sweet the answer Echo makes
　　To music at night,
When, roused by lute or horn, she wakes,
And, far away, o'er lawns and lakes,
　　Goes answering light.

Yet Love hath echoes truer far,
　　And far more sweet,
Than e'er beneath the moonlight's star,
Or horn or lute, or soft guitar,
　　The songs repeat.

'Tis when the sigh, in youth sincere,
　　And only then,—
The sigh that's breathed for one to hear,
Is by that one, that only dear,
　　Breathed back again.

THOUGH I AM YOUNG
AND CANNOT TELL

BEN JONSON
(1572–1637)

Though I am young, and cannot tell
   Either what Death or Love is well,
Yet I have heard they both bear darts,
   And both do aim at human hearts.
And then again, I have been told
   Love wounds with heat, as Death with cold;
So that I fear they do but bring
   Extremes to touch, and mean one thing.

As in a ruin we it call
   One thing to be blown up, or fall;
Or to our end like way may have
   By a flash of lightning, or a wave;
So Love's inflamèd shaft or brand
   May kill as soon as Death's cold hand;
Except Love's fires the virtue have
   To fright the frost out of the grave.

THE YOUNG HOUSEWIFE

William Carlos Williams
(1883–1963)

At ten A.M. the young housewife
moves about in negligee behind
the wooden walls of her husband's house.
I pass solitary in my car.

Then again she comes to the curb
to call the ice-man, fish-man, and stands
shy, uncorseted, tucking in
stray ends of hair, and I compare her
to a fallen leaf.

The noiseless wheels of my car
rush with a crackling sound over
dried leaves as I bow and pass smiling.

BLUE GIRLS

John Crowe Ransom
(1888–1974)

Twirling your blue skirts, travelling the sward
Under the towers of your seminary,
Go listen to your teachers old and contrary
Without believing a word.

Tie the white fillets then about your hair
And think no more of what will come to pass
Than bluebirds that go walking on the grass
And chattering on the air.

Practise your beauty, blue girls, before it fail;
And I will cry with my loud lips and publish
Beauty which all our power shall never
    establish,
It is so frail.

For I could tell you a story which is true;
I know a lady with a terrible tongue,
Blear eyes fallen from blue,
All her perfections tarnished—yet it is not long
Since she was lovelier than any of you.

MY LADY'S PRESENCE MAKES
THE ROSES RED

HENRY CONSTABLE
(1562–1613)

My lady's presence makes the roses red,
    Because to see her lips they blush with
        shame.
    The lily's leaves for envy pale became,
And her white hands in them this envy bred.
The marigold the leaves abroad doth spread,
    Because the sun's and her power is the same.
    The violet of purple colour came,
Dyed in the blood she made my heart to shed.
    In brief, all flowers from her their virtue
        take;
From her sweet breath their sweet smells do
        proceed;
    The living heat which her eyebeams doth
        make
Warmeth the ground and quickeneth the seed.
    The rain wherewith she watereth the
        flowers,
    Falls from mine eyes which she dissolves in
        showers.

TO MY DEAR AND LOVING HUSBAND

ANNE BRADSTREET
(1612?–1672)

If ever two were one, then surely we.
If ever man were loved by wife, then thee;
If ever wife was happy in a man,
Compare with me, ye women, if you can.
I prize thy love more than whole mines of gold
Or all the riches that the East doth hold.
My love is such that rivers cannot quench,
Nor ought but love from thee, give
    recompense.
Thy love is such I can no way repay,
The heavens reward thee manifold, I pray.
Then while we live, in love let's so persevere
That when we live no more, we may live ever.

FRESH SPRING, THE HERALD OF LOVE'S MIGHTY KING

Edmund Spenser
(1552–1599)

Fresh Spring, the herald of Love's mighty King,
  In whose cote-armour richly are display'd
All sorts of flowers the which on earth do
    spring
  In goodly colours gloriously array'd,—
  Go to my Love, where she is careless laid
Yet in her Winter's bower not well awake:
  Tell her the joyous time will not be stay'd
Unless she do him by the fore-lock take:
Bid her therefore herself soon ready make:
  To wait on Love amongst his lovely crew:
Where every one that misseth then her make,
  Shall be by him amerced with penance due.
    Make haste therefore, sweet Love, whilst it
      is prime,
    For none can call again the passèd time.

MEN LOVED WHOLLY BEYOND WISDOM

Louise Bogan
(1897–1970)

Men loved wholly beyond wisdom
Have the staff without the banner.
Like a fire in a dry thicket,
Rising within women's eyes
Is the love men must return.
Heart, so subtle now, and trembling,
What a marvel to be wise,
To love never in this manner!
To be quiet in the fern
Like a thing gone dead and still,
Listening to the prisoned cricket
Shake its terrible, dissembling
Music in the granite hill.

TO MEMORY

MARY COLERIDGE
(1861–1907)

Strange power, I know not what thou art,
Murderer or mistress of my heart.
I know I'd rather meet the blow
Of my most unrelenting foe
Than live—as I live now—to be
Slain twenty times a day by thee.

Yet, when I would command thee hence,
Thou mockest at the vain pretence,
Murmuring in my ear a song
Once loved, alas! forgotten long;
And on my brow I feel a kiss
That I would rather die than miss.

SONG

WILLIAM BLAKE
(1757–1827)

How sweet I roam'd from field to field,
   And tasted all the summer's pride,
'Till I the prince of love beheld,
   Who in the sunny beams did glide!

He shew'd me lilies for my hair,
   And blushing roses for my brow;
He led me through his gardens fair,
   Where all his golden pleasures grow.

With sweet May dews my wings were wet,
   And Phoebus fir'd my vocal rage;
He caught me in his silken net,
   And shut me in his golden cage.

He loves to sit and hear me sing,
   Then, laughing, sports and plays with me;
Then stretches out my golden wing,
   And mocks my loss of liberty.

TIME

Thomas Lux
(1946–   )

I have a friend whose hair is like time: dark
deranged coils lit by a lamp
when she bends back her head to laugh. A
    unique event,
such as the crucifixion of Christ, was not
subject to repetition, thought St. Augustine,
    and therefore,
time is linear. Does the universe
have an end, a beginning? Yes, the former the
    door
through which she departs, the latter
the door by which she returns,
and inbetween there is no rest from wanting
    her.

Time—each moment of which a hair on a
    child's nape.
Time—the chain between the churning tractor
    and the stump.
Time—her gown tossed like a continent at the
    creation.
Newton, an absolutist, thought time a container
in which the universe exists—nonending,
    nonbeginning.

Time—enamored, forgiven by dust
and capable of calling a single blade of grass an
  oasis.
Time—of swivel, small streams, plinth,
  stanchions.
And then Kant says, no, time does not apply
to the universe, only to the way we think
  about time.

Time—the spot where the violin touches the
  maestro's cheek.
Time—an endless range of cumulonimbus.
Time—Good Monarch of the deepest blue
  inevitable.
The relativists (with whom the absolutists,
as usual, disagree) argue that concepts of past,
present, and future are mind dependent, i.e.,
would time exist without conscious beings?
Oh Ultimate Abstract, is there time
in time, is there rest, in time,
from wanting her?

MY GRANDMOTHER'S
LOVE LETTERS

HART CRANE
(1899–1932)

There are no stars to-night
But those of memory.
Yet how much room for memory there is
In the loose girdle of soft rain.

There is even room enough
For the letters of my mother's mother,
Elizabeth,
That have been pressed so long
Into a corner of the roof
That they are brown and soft,
And liable to melt as snow.

Over the greatness of such space
Steps must be gentle.
It is all hung by an invisible white hair.
It trembles as birch limbs webbing the air.

And I ask myself:

"Are your fingers long enough to play
Old keys that are but echoes:
Is the silence strong enough
To carry back the music to its source
And back to you again
As though to her?"

Yet I would lead my grandmother by the hand
Through much of what she would not understand;
And so I stumble. And the rain continues on the roof
With such a sound of gently pitying laughter.

AGE TO YOUTH

JUDITH WRIGHT
(1915–   )

The sooty bush in the park
is green as any forest
for the boy to lie beneath,
with his arms around his dearest;

the black of the back street
is washed as any cloud
when the girl and the boy
touch hands among the crowd.

No, nothing's better than love,
than to want and to hold:
it is wise in the young
to forget the common world:

to be lost in the flesh
and the light shining there:
not to listen to the old
whose tune is fear and care—

who tell them love's a drink
poisoned with sorrow,
the flesh a flower today
and withered by tomorrow.

It is wise in the young
to let heart go racing heart,
to believe that the earth
is young and safe and sweet;

and the message we should send
from age back to youth
is that every kiss and glance
is truer than the truth;

that whatever we repent
of the time that we live,
it is never what we give—
it is never that we love.

GIVE ALL TO LOVE

RALPH WALDO EMERSON
(1803–1882)

Give all to love;
Obey thy heart;
Friends, kindred, days,
Estate, good-fame,
Plans, credit and the Muse,—
Nothing refuse.

'T is a brave master;
Let it have scope:
Follow it utterly,
Hope beyond hope:
High and more high
It dives into noon,
With wing unspent,
Untold intent:
But it is a god,
Knows its own path
And the outlets of the sky.

It was never for the mean;
It requireth courage stout.
Souls above doubt,
Valor unbending,
It will reward,—
They shall return
More than they were,
And ever ascending.

Leave all for love;
Yet, hear me, yet,
One word more thy heart behoved,
One pulse more of firm endeavor,—
Keep thee to-day,
To-morrow, forever,
Free as an Arab
Of thy beloved.

Cling with life to the maid;
But when the surprise,
First vague shadow of surmise
Flits across her bosom young,
Of a joy apart from thee,
Free be she, fancy-free;
Nor thou detain her vesture's hem,
Nor the palest rose she flung
From her summer diadem.

Though thou loved her as thyself,
As a self of purer clay,
Though her parting dims the day,
Stealing grace from all alive;
Heartily know,
When half-gods go,
The gods arrive.

THE COLUMBINE

Jones Very
(1813–1880)

Still, still my eye will gaze long fixed on
    thee,
Till I forget that I am called a man,
And at thy side fast-rooted seem to be,
And the breeze comes my cheek with thine
    to fan.
Upon this craggy hill our life shall pass,
A life of summer days and summer joys,
Nodding our honey-bells mid pliant grass
In which the bee half hid his time employs;
And here we'll drink with thirsty pores the
    rain,
And turn dew-sprinkled to the rising sun,
And look when in the flaming west again
His orb across the heaven its path has run;
Here left in darkness on the rocky steep,
My weary eyes shall close like folding flowers
    in sleep.

IF I WERE TICKLED BY
THE RUB OF LOVE

DYLAN THOMAS
(1914–1953)

If I were tickled by the rub of love,
A rooking girl who stole me for her side,
Broke through her straws, breaking my
    bandaged string,
If the red tickle as the cattle calve
Still set to scratch a laughter from my lung,
I would not fear the apple nor the flood
Nor the bad blood of spring.

Shall it be male or female? say the cells,
And drop the plum like fire from the flesh.
If I were tickled by the hatching hair,
The winging bone that sprouted in the heels,
The itch of man upon the baby's thigh,
I would not fear the gallows nor the axe
Nor the crossed sticks of war.

Shall it be male or female? say the fingers
That chalk the walls with green girls and their
    men.
I would not fear the muscling-in of love
If I were tickled by the urchin hungers
Rehearsing heat upon a raw-edged nerve.
I would not fear the devil in the loin
Nor the outspoken grave.

If I were tickled by the lovers' rub
That wipes away not crow's-foot nor the lock
Of sick old manhood on the fallen jaws,
Time and the crabs and the sweethearting crib
Would leave me cold as butter for the flies,
The sea of scums could drown me as it broke
Dead on the sweethearts' toes.

This world is half the devil's and my own,
Daft with the drug that's smoking in a girl
And curling round the bud that forks her eye.
An old man's shank one-marrowed with my
    bone,
And all the herrings smelling in the sea,
I sit and watch the worm beneath my nail
Wearing the quick away.

And that's the rub, the only rub that tickles.
The knobbly ape that swings along his sex
From damp love-darkness and the nurse's twist
Can never raise the midnight of a chuckle,
Nor when he finds a beauty in the breast
Of lover, mother, lovers, or his six
Feet in the rubbing dust.

And what's the rub? Death's feather on the
    nerve?
Your mouth, my love, the thistle in the kiss?
My Jack of Christ born thorny on the tree?

The words of death are dryer than his stiff,
My wordy wounds are printed with your hair.
I would be tickled by the rub that is:
Man be my metaphor.

MEDIOCRITY IN LOVE REJECTED

THOMAS CAREW
(1595?–1640?)

Give me more love, or more disdain;
    The torrid or the frozen zone
Bring equal ease unto my pain;
    The temperate affords me none:
Either extreme, of love or hate,
Is sweeter than a calm estate.

Give me a storm; if it be love,
    Like Danaë in that golden shower,
I swim in pleasure; if it prove
    Disdain, that torrent will devour
My vulture hopes; and he's possessed
Of heaven that's but from hell released.
    Then crown my joys, or cure my pain;
    Give me more love or more disdain.

LORD RANDAL

UNKNOWN

(c. 15th Century)

'O where hae ye been, Lord Randal, my son?
O where hae ye been, my handsome young
  man?'
'I hae been to the wild wood; mother make my
  bed soon,
For I'm weary wi' hunting, and fain wad lie
  down.'

'Where gat ye your dinner, Lord Randal, my
  son?
Where gat ye your dinner, my handsome young
  man?'
'I dined with my true-love; mother make my
  bed soon,
For I'm weary wi' hunting, and fain wad lie
  down.'

'What gat ye to your dinner, Lord Randal, my
  son?
What gat ye to your dinner, my handsome
  young man?'
'I gat eels boiled in broth; mother make my bed
  soon,
For I'm weary wi' hunting, and fain wad lie
  down.'

'And wha gat your leavings, Lord Randal, my
    son?
And wha gat your leavings, my handsome
    young man?'
'My hawks and my hounds; mother make my
    bed soon,
For I'm weary wi' hunting and fain wad lie
    down.'

'What became of your bloodhounds, Lord
    Randal, my son?
What became of your bloodhounds, my
    handsome young man?'
'O they swelled and they died; mother make
    my bed soon,
For I'm weary wi' hunting, and fain wad lie
    down.'

'O I fear ye are poisoned, Lord Randal, my son!
O I fear ye are poisoned, my handsome young
    man!'
'O yes! I am poisoned; mother make my bed
    soon,
For I'm sick at the heart and I fain wad lie
    down.'

LOVE WITHOUT HOPE

ROBERT GRAVES
(1895–1985)

Love without hope, as when the young bird-
  catcher
Swept off his tall hat to the Squire's own
  daughter,
So let the imprisoned larks escape and fly
Singing about her head, as she rode by.

PORTRAIT OF A LADY

William Carlos Williams
(1883–1963)

Your thighs are appletrees
whose blossoms touch the sky.
Which sky? The sky
where Watteau hung a lady's
slipper. Your knees
are a southern breeze—or
a gust of snow. Agh! what
sort of man was Fragonard?
—as if that answered
anything. Ah, yes—below
the knees, since the tune
drops that way, it is
one of those white summer days,
the tall grass of your ankles
flickers upon the shore—
Which shore?—
the sand clings to my lips—
Which shore?
Agh, petals maybe. How
should I know?
Which shore? Which shore?
I said petals from an appletree.

WHY CAN'T I LEAVE YOU?

Ai
(1947–   )

You stand behind the old black mare,
dressed as always in that red shirt,
stained from sweat, the crying of the armpits,
that will not stop for anything,
stroking her rump, while the barley goes
    unplanted.
I pick up my suitcase and set it down,
as I try to leave you again.
I smooth the hair back from your forehead.
I think with your laziness and the drought too,
you'll be needing my help more than ever.
You take my hands, I nod
and go to the house to unpack,
having found another reason to stay.

I undress, then put on my white lace slip
for you to take off, because you like that
and when you come in, you pull down the straps
and I unbutton your shirt.
I know we can't give each other any more
or any less than what we have.
There is safety in that, so much
that I can never get past the packing,
the begging you to please, if I can't make you
    happy,
come close between my thighs
and let me laugh for you from my second mouth.

AS A POSSIBLE LOVER

AMIRI BARAKA
(1934–   )

Practices
silence, the way of wind
bursting
its early lull. Cold morning
to night, we go so
slowly, without
thought
to ourselves. (Enough
to have thought
tonight, nothing
finishes it. What
you are, will have
no certainty, or
end. That you will
stay, where you are,
a human gentle wisp
of life. Ah . . .)
        practices
loneliness,
as a virtue. A single
specious need
to keep
what you have
never really
had.

I CARE NOT FOR THESE LADIES

THOMAS CAMPION
(1567–1620)

I care not for these ladies,
That must be wooed and prayed:
Give me kind Amaryllis,
The wanton country maid.
Nature art disdaineth,
Her beauty is her own.
    Her when we court and kiss,
    She cries, "Forsooth, let go!"
    But when we come where comfort is,
    She never will say no.

If I love Amaryllis,
She gives me fruit and flowers:
But if we love these ladies,
We must give golden showers.
Give them gold, that sell love,
Give me the nut-brown lass,
    Who, when we court and kiss,
    She cries, "Forsooth, let go!"
    But when we come where comfort is,
    She never will say no.

These ladies must have pillows,
And beds by strangers wrought;
Give me a bower of willows,
Of moss and leaves unbought,
And fresh Amaryllis,
With milk and honey fed;
 Who, when we court and kiss,
 She cries, "Forsooth, let go!"
 But when we come where comfort is,
 She never will say no.

WHEN, WITH YOU ASLEEP

Juan Ramon Jimenez
(1881–1958)

When, with you asleep, I plunge into your soul,
and I listen, with my ear
on your naked breast,
to your tranquil heart, it seems to me
that, in its deep throbbing, I surprise
the secret of the center
of the world.

It seems to me
that legions of angels
on celestial steeds
—as when, in the height
of the night we listen, without a breath
and our ears to the earth,
to distant hoofbeats that never arrive—,
that legions of angels
are coming through you, from afar
—like the Three Kings
to the eternal birth
of our love—,
they are coming through you, from afar,
to bring me, in your dreams,
the secret of the center
of the heavens.

TRANSLATED BY PERRY HIGMAN

THE GOOD-MORROW

JOHN DONNE
(1572–1631)

I wonder, by my troth, what thou and I
Did till we loved. Were we not weaned till
    then,
But sucked on country pleasures, childishly?
Or snorted we in the seven sleepers' den?
'Twas so; but this, all pleasures fancies be.
If ever any beauty I did see,
Which I desired and got, 'twas but a dream of
    thee.

And now good-morrow to our waking souls,
Which watch not one another out of fear;
For love all love of other sights controls
And makes one little room an everywhere.
Let sea-discoverers to new worlds have gone,
Let maps to others worlds on worlds have
    shown,
Let us possess one world, each hath one, and is
    one.

My face in thine eye, thine in mine appears,
And true plain hearts do in the faces rest,
Where can we find two better hemispheres
Without sharp North, without declining West?
Whatever dies was not mixed equally;
If our two loves be one, or thou and I
Love so alike that none do slacken, none can
    die.

TO JANE: THE KEEN STARS WERE TWINKLING

PERCY BYSSHE SHELLEY
(1792–1822)

1

The keen stars were twinkling,
And the fair moon was rising among them,
   Dear Jane!
The guitar was tinkling,
But the notes were not sweet till you sung
them
    Again.

2

As the moon's soft splendor
O'er the faint cold starlight of Heaven
   Is thrown,
So your voice most tender
To the strings without soul had then given
   Its own.

3

The stars will awaken,
Though the moon sleep a full hour later,
    Tonight;
    No leaf will be shaken
Whilst the dews of your melody scatter
    Delight.

4

    Though the sound overpowers,
Sing again, with your dear voice revealing
    A tone
    Of some world far from ours,
Where music and moonlight and feeling
    Are one.

FAIREST ISLE

John Dryden
(1631–1700)

Fairest isle, all isles excelling,
    Seat of pleasures and of loves;
Venus here will choose her dwelling,
    And forsake her Cyprian groves.

Cupid from his favourite nation
    Care and envy will remove;
Jealousy, that poisons passion,
    And despair, that dies for love.

Gentle murmurs, sweet complaining,
    Sighs that blow the fire of love;
Soft repulses, kind disdaining,
    Shall be all the pains you prove.

Every swain shall pay his duty,
    Grateful every nymph shall prove;
And as these excel in beauty,
    Those shall be renowned for love.

GREEN, GREEN, AND GREEN AGAIN . . .

CONRAD AIKEN
(1889–1973)

Green, green, and green again, and greener
     still,
spring towards summer bends the immortal
     bow,
and northward breaks the wave of daffodil,
and northward breaks the wave of summer's
     snow:
green, green, and green again, and greener yet,
wide as this forest is, which counts its leaves,
wide as this kingdom, in a green sea set,
which round its shores perpetual blossom
     weaves—
green, green, and green again, and green once
     more,
the season finds its term—then greenest, even,
when frost at twilight on the leaf lies hoar,
and one cold star shines bright in greenest
     heaven:
but love, like music, keeps no seasons ever;
like music, too, once known is known forever.

THE CLAIM THAT HAS THE CANKER ON THE ROSE

JOSEPH PLUNKETT
(1887–1916)

The claim that has the canker on the rose
Is mine on you, man's claim on Paradise
Hopelessly lost that ceaselessly he sighs
And all unmerited God still bestows;
The claim on the invisible wind that blows
The flame of charity to enemies
Not to the deadliest sinners, God denies—
Less claim than this have I on you, God knows.
I cannot ask for any thing from you
Because my pride is eaten up with shame
That you should think my poverty a claim
Upon your charity, knowing it is true
That all the glories formerly I knew
Shone from the cloudy splendour of your name.

PETER QUINCE AT THE CLAVIER

WALLACE STEVENS
(1879–1955)

I

Just as my fingers on these keys
Make music, so the selfsame sounds
On my spirit make a music, too.

Music is feeling, then, not sound;
And thus it is that what I feel,
Here in this room, desiring you,

Thinking of your blue-shadowed silk,
Is music. It is like the strain
Waked in the elders by Susanna.

Of a green evening, clear and warm,
She bathed in her still garden, while
The red-eyed elders watching, felt

The basses of their beings throb
In witching chords, and their thin blood
Pulse pizzicati of Hosanna.

II

In the green water, clear and warm,
Susanna lay.
She searched
The touch of springs,
And found
Concealed imaginings.
She sighed,
For so much melody.

Upon the bank, she stood
In the cool
Of spent emotions.
She felt, among the leaves,
The dew
Of old devotions.

She walked upon the grass,
Still quavering.
The winds were like her maids,
On timid feet,
Fetching her woven scarves,
Yet wavering.

A breath upon her hand
Muted the night.
She turned—
A cymbal crashed,
And roaring horns.

III

Soon, with a noise like tambourines,
Came her attendant Byzantines.

They wondered why Susanna cried
Against the elders by her side;

And as they whispered, the refrain
Was like a willow swept by rain.

Anon, their lamps' uplifted flame
Revealed Susanna and her shame.

And then, the simpering Byzantines
Fled, with a noise like tambourines.

IV

Beauty is momentary in the mind—
The fitful tracing of a portal;
But in the flesh it is immortal.
The body dies; the body's beauty lives.
So evenings die, in their green going,
A wave, interminably flowing.
So gardens die, their meek breath scenting
The cowl of winter, done repenting.
So maidens die, to the auroral
Celebration of a maiden's choral.
Susanna's music touched the bawdy strings
Of those white elders; but, escaping,
Left only Death's ironic scraping.
Now, in its immortality, it plays
On the clear viol of her memory,
And makes a constant sacrament of praise.

THIS LUNAR BEAUTY

W. H. AUDEN
(1907–1973)

This lunar beauty
Has no history,
Is complete and early;
If beauty later
Bear any feature,
It had a lover
And is another.

This like a dream
Keeps other time,
And daytime is
The loss of this;
For time is inches
And the heart's changes,
Where ghost has haunted
Lost and wanted.

But this was never
A ghost's endeavour
Nor, finished this,
Was ghost at ease;
And till it pass
Love shall not near
The sweetness here,
Nor sorrow take
His endless look.

EMILY DICKINSON
(1830–1886)

To make a prairie it takes a clover and one bee,
One clover, and a bee,
And revery.
The revery alone will do,
If bees are few.

NO, NO, FAIR HERETIC

SIR JOHN SUCKLING
(1609–1642)

No, no, fair heretic, it needs must be
   But an ill love in me,
   And worse for thee;
For were it in my power,
To love thee now this hour
   More than I did the last;
I would then so fall
    I might not love at all;
Love that can flow, and can admit increase,
Admits as well an ebb, and may grow less.

True love is still the same; the Torrid Zones,
   And those more frigid ones
   It must not know:
For love grown cold or hot,
   Is lust or friendship, not
   The thing we have.
For that's a flame would die
    Held down, or up too high:
Then think I love more than I can express,
And would love more could I but love thee less.

OPEN HOUSE

THEODORE ROETHKE
(1908–1963)

My secrets cry aloud.
I have no need for tongue.
My heart keeps open house,
My doors are widely swung.
An epic of the eyes
My love, with no disguise.

My truths are all foreknown,
This anguish self-revealed.
I'm naked to the bone,
With nakedness my shield.
Myself is what I wear:
I keep the spirit spare.

The anger will endure,
The deed will speak the truth
In language strict and pure.
I stop the lying mouth:
Rage warps my clearest cry
To witless agony.

SONNET 147

WILLIAM SHAKESPEARE
(1564–1616)

My love is as a fever, longing still
For that which longer nurseth the disease;
Feeding on that which doth preserve the ill,
The uncertain sickly appetite to please.
My reason, the physician to my love,
Angry that his prescriptions are not kept,
Hath left me, and I desperate now approve
Desire is death, which physic did except.
Past cure I am, now Reason is past care,
And frantic-mad with evermore unrest;
My thoughts and my discourse as madmen's
    are,
At random from the truth vainly express'd;
    For I have sworn thee fair, and thought thee
    bright,
    Who art as black as hell, as dark as night.

WHY ART THOU SILENT!

William Wordsworth
(1770–1850)

Why art thou silent! Is thy love a plant
Of such weak fibre that the treacherous air
Of absence withers what was once so fair?
Is there no debt to pay, no boon to grant?
Yet have my thoughts for thee been vigilant—
Bound to thy service with unceasing care,
The mind's least generous wish a mendicant
For nought but what thy happiness could spare.
Speak—though this soft warm heart, once free
   to hold
A thousand tender pleasures, thine and mine,
Be left more desolate, more dreary cold
Than a forsaken bird's-nest filled with snow
'Mid its own bush of leafless eglantine—
Speak, that my torturing doubts their end may
   know!

A BROKEN APPOINTMENT

THOMAS HARDY
(1840–1928)

You did not come,
And marching Time drew on, and wore me
  numb.
Yet less for loss of your dear presence there
Than that I thus found lacking in your make
That high compassion which can overbear
Reluctance for pure lovingkindness' sake
Grieved I, when, as the hope-hour stroked its
  sum,
      You did not come.

      You love not me,
And love alone can lend you loyalty;
—I know and knew it. But, unto the store
Of human deeds divine in all but name,
Was it not worth a little hour or more
To add yet this: Once you, a woman, came
To soothe a time-torn man; even though it be
      You love not me?

if i have made,my lady,intricate

e. e. cummings
(1894–1962)

if i have made,my lady,intricate
imperfect various things chiefly which wrong
your eyes (frailer than most deep dreams are frail)
songs less firm than your body's whitest song
upon my mind—if i have failed to snare
the glance too shy—if through my singing slips
the very skillful strangeness of your smile
the keen primeval silence of your hair

—let the world say "his most wise music stole
nothing from death"—
                                        you only will create
(who are so perfectly alive) my shame:
lady through whose profound and fragile lips
the sweet small clumsy feet of April came

into the ragged meadow of my soul.

HOW STRANGE LOVE IS,
IN EVERY STATE OF CONSCIOUSNESS

DELMORE SCHWARTZ
(1913–1966)

How strange love is in every kind of
    consciousness:
How strange it is that only such gentleness
Begets the fury of joy and all its tenderness,
That lips and hands for all their littleness
Can move throughout the body's wilderness
Beyond the gaze of consciousness, however it
    towers
Possessed and blessed by the power which
    flowers as a fountain flowers!

WELL WATER

RANDALL JARRELL
(1914–1965)

What a girl called 'the dailiness of life'
(Adding an errand to your errand. Saying,
'Since you're up . . .' Making you a means to
A means to a means to) is well water
Pumped from an old well at the bottom of the
    world.
The pump you pump the water from is rusty
And hard to move and absurd, a squirrel-wheel
A sick squirrel turns slowly, through the sunny
Inexorable hours. And yet sometimes
The wheel turns of its own weight, the rusty
Pump pumps over your sweating face the clear
Water, cold, so cold! you cup your hands
And gulp from them the dailiness of life.

THE STRANGER

JEAN GARRIGUE
(1914–1972)

Now upon this piteous year
I sit in Denmark beside the quai
And nothing that the fishers say
Or the children carrying boats
Can recall me from that place
Where sense and wish departed me
Whose very shores take on
The whiteness of anon.
For I beheld a stranger there
Who moved ahead of me
So tensile and so dancer made
That like a thief I followed her
Though my heart was so alive
I thought it equal to that beauty.
But when at last a turning came
Like the branching of a river
And I saw if she walked on
She would be gone forever,
Fear, then, so wounded me
As fell upon my ear
The voice a blind man dreams
And broke on me the smile
I dreamed as deaf men hear,
I stood there like a spy,
My tongue and eyelids taken
In such necessity.

Now upon this piteous year
The rains of Autumn fall.
Where may she be?
I suffered her to disappear
Who hunger in the prison of my fear.
That lean and brown, that stride,
That cold and melting pride,
For whom the river like a clear
Melodic line and the distant carrousel
Where lovers on their beasts of play
Rose and fell,
That wayfare where the swan adorned
With every wave and eddy
The honor of his sexual beauty,
Create her out of sorrow
That, never perishing,
Is a stately thing.

THE TROLL'S NOSEGAY

ROBERT GRAVES
(1895–1985)

A simple nosegay! was that much to ask?
(Winter still nagged, with scarce a bud yet
   showing.)
He loved her ill, if he resigned the task.
'Somewhere,' she cried, 'there *must* be blossom
   blowing.'
It seems my lady wept and the troll swore
By Heaven he hated tears: he'd cure her
   spleen—
Where she had begged one flower he'd shower
   fourscore,
A bunch fit to amaze a China Queen.

Cold fog-drawn Lily, pale mist-magic Rose
He conjured, and in a glassy cauldron set
With elvish unsubstantial Mignonette
And such vague bloom as wandering dreams
   enclose.
But she?
      Awed,
           Charmed to tears,
              Distracted,
                 Yet—
Even yet, perhaps, a trifle piqued—who
   knows?

THE WILD HONEY SUCKLE

PHILIP FRENEAU
(1752–1832)

Fair flower, that dost so comely grow,
Hid in this silent, dull retreat,
Untouched thy honied blossoms blow,
Unseen thy little branches greet:
   No roving foot shall crush thee here,
   No busy hand provoke a tear.

By Nature's self in white arrayed,
She bade thee shun the vulgar eye,
And planted here the guardian shade,
And sent soft waters murmuring by;
   Thus quietly thy summer goes,
   Thy days declining to repose.

Smit with those charms, that must decay,
I grieve to see your future doom;
They died—nor were those flowers more gay,
The flowers that did in Eden bloom;
   Unpitying frosts, and Autumn's power
   Shall leave no vestige of this flower.

From morning suns and evening dews
At first thy little being came:
If nothing once, you nothing lose,
For when you die you are the same;
   The space between, is but an hour,
   The frail duration of a flower.

ONE DAY I WROTE HER NAME UPON THE STRAND

EDMUND SPENSER
(1552–1599)

One day I wrote her name upon the strand,
But came the waves and washed it away:
Agayne I wrote it with a second hand,
But came the tyde, and made my paynes his
  pray.
Vayne man, sayd she, that doest in vaine assay,
A mortall thing so to immortalize,
For I my selve shall lyke to this decay,
And eek my name bee wyped out lykewize.
Not so, (quod I) let baser things devize
To dy in dust, but you shall live by fame:
My verse your vertues rare shall eternize,
And in the hevens wryte your glorious name.
Where whenas death shall al the world subdew,
Our love shall live, and later life renew.

I GAVE MYSELF TO HIM

EMILY DICKINSON
(1830–1886)

I gave myself to him,
And took himself for pay.
The solemn contract of a life
Was ratified this way.

The wealth might disappoint,
Myself a poorer prove
Than this great purchaser suspect,
The daily own of Love

Depreciate the vision;
But, till the merchant buy,
Still fable, in the isles of spice,
The subtle cargoes lie.

At least, 't is mutual risk,—
Some found it mutual gain;
Sweet debt of Life,—each night to owe,
Insolvent, every noon.

TO ANTHEA WHO MAY COMMAND
HIM ANYTHING

ROBERT HERRICK
(1591–1674)

Bid me to live, and I will live
   Thy Protestant to be:
Or bid me love, and I will give
   A loving heart to thee.

A heart as soft, a heart as kind,
   A heart as sound and free
As in the whole world thou canst find,
   That heart I'll give to thee.

Bid that heart stay, and it will stay,
   To honour thy decree:
Or bid it languish quite away,
   And 't shall do so for thee.

Bid me weep, and I will weep
   While I have eyes to see:
And, having none, yet I will keep
   A heart to weep for thee.

Bid me despair, and I'll despair
   Under that cypress tree:
Or bid me die, and I will dare
   E'en death to die for thee.

Thou art my life, my love, my heart,
  The very eyes of me,
Thou hast command of every part,
  To live and die for thee.

THERE ARE DELICACIES

EARLE BIRNEY
(1904–   )

there are delicacies in you
    like the hearts of watches
there are wheels that turn
    on the tips of rubies
& tiny intricate locks

i need your help
    to contrive keys
there is so little time
    even for the finest
    of watches

ONE WORD IS TOO OFTEN PROFANED

PERCY BYSSHE SHELLEY
(1792–1822)

One word is too often profaned
    For me to profane it,
One feeling too falsely disdained
    For thee to disdain it;
One hope is too like despair
    For prudence to smother,
And pity from thee more dear
    Than that from another.

I can give not what men call love,
    But wilt thou accept not
The worship the heart lifts above
    And the heavens reject not,—
The desire of the moth for the star,
    Of the night for the morrow,
The devotion to something afar
    From the sphere of our sorrow?

A QUESTION

John Millington Synge
(1871–1909)

I asked if I got sick and died, would you
With my black funeral go walking too,
If you'd stand close to hear them talk or pray
While I'm let down in that steep bank of clay.

And, No, you said, for if you saw a crew
Of living idiots pressing round that new
Oak coffin—they alive, I dead beneath
That board—you'd rave and rend them with
   your teeth.

AT BAIA

H.D. (HILDA DOOLITTLE)
(1886–1961)

I should have thought
in a dream you would have brought
some lovely, perilous thing,
orchids piled in a great sheath,
as who would say (in a dream),
"I send you this,
who left the blue veins
of your throat unkissed."

Why was it that your hands
(that never took mine),
your hands that I could see
drift over the orchid-heads
so carefully,
your hands, so fragile, sure to lift
so gently, the fragile flower-stuff—
ah, ah, how was it

You never sent (in a dream)
the very form, the very scent,
not heavy, not sensuous,
but perilous—perilous—
of orchids, piled in a great sheath,
and folded underneath on a bright scroll,
some word:

"Flower sent to flower;
for white hands, the lesser white,
less lovely of flower-leaf,"

or

"Lover to lover, no kiss,
no touch, but forever and ever this."

DISTRACTED

PEDRO SALINAS
(1891–1951)

You are no longer here. What I see
of you, body, is shadow, deceit.
Your soul has gone away
where you will go tomorrow.
Yet even this afternoon offers me
false hostages, vague smiles,
slow gestures,
an already distracted love.
But your intention of going
took you where you wanted,
far from here, where you are
saying to me:
"Here I am with you, look."
And you show me your absence.

TRANSLATED BY PERRY HIGMAN

PUBLIC TELEVISION

Eileen Myles
(1949–   )

I'm always scared. Aren't
you. In the kitchen
everything is humming,
my mother comments
that what I'm reading
looks heavy. I say
it isn't it's
about television
and go on
to explain
structuralism &
Robert Young
& mention
Zeborah in
passing as
where I
got this
book—
and that's
all my
mother
heard, I
know it.

I don't
know
why you're
not calling
me this
morning.

Is it because
I only wrote
you one love
poem last
August or
is it that
you're ashamed of
me I
fume up the
small winding
hills of Man-
chester, Mass.

There but
for the
grace of
god go
I behind
a woman
my age
dragging
her two
children.

I hurry
home to
remember
which postcard
I forgot
to send.
Can I be
breezy in
a letter?

My mother's
gonna sit
by the
stove. It's
cold in
the kitchen
in New
England.

The sportscasters
are funny
here & the
people eat
a lot and
aren't so
friendly but
they say
hello.

If you
haven't
called me
that does
mean some-
thing. That
I should
mind my
own business
the new
way to
be. There
is of course
a mass media,
the thing
that everyone
sees that
everyone knows
what does
everyone
know, do
they care?
Does it look
okay. Then
there's the
little private
world of
feelings, let's
call that
access.

I don't care
how it
looks, or
if we're
watched by
how many
billion viewers,
see, I am concerned
with having
the important
spot in
your heart
and a channel
to mine
I want
this beam
to be
long and
strong
and true.
Is it?

O WORLD, THOU CHOOSEST NOT THE BETTER PART

GEORGE SANTAYANA
(1863–1952)

O world, thou choosest not the better part!
It is not wisdom to be only wise,
And on the inward vision close the eyes,
But it is wisdom to believe the heart.
Columbus found a world, and had no chart,
Save one that faith deciphered in the skies;
To trust the soul's invincible surmise
Was all his science and his only art.
Our knowledge is a torch of smoky pine
That lights the pathway but one step ahead
Across a void of mystery and dread.
Bid, then, the tender light of faith to shine
By which alone the mortal heart is led
Unto the thinking of the thought divine.

WINTER REMEMBERED

JOHN CROWE RANSOM
(1888–1974)

Two evils, monstrous either one apart,
Possessed me, and were long and loath at going:
A cry of Absence, Absence, in the heart,
And in the wood the furious winter blowing.

Think not, when fire was bright upon my
    bricks,
And past the tight boards hardly a wind could
    enter,
I glowed like them, the simple burning sticks,
Far from my cause, my proper heat and center.

Better to walk forth in the frozen air
And wash my wound in the snows; that would
    be healing;
Because my heart would throb less painful
    there,
Being caked with cold, and past the smart of
    feeling.

And where I walked, the murderous winter
    blast
Would have this body bowed, these eyeballs
    streaming,
And though I think this heart's blood froze not
    fast
It ran too small to spare one drop for
    dreaming.

Dear love, these fingers that had known your
    touch,
And tied our separate forces first together,
Were ten poor idiot fingers not worth much,
Ten frozen parsnips hanging in the weather.

PUSHKIN TOWN

From The Life of Towns

ANNE CARSON
(1950–   )

When I live I live in the ancient future.
Deep rivers run to it angel pavements are in
    use.
It has rules.
And love.
And the first rule is.
The love of chance.
Some words of yours are very probably ore
    there.
Or will be by the time our eyes are ember.

COMPENSATION

PAUL LAURENCE DUNBAR
(1872–1906)

Because I had loved so deeply,
    Because I had loved so long,
God in His great compassion
    Gave me the gift of song.

Because I have loved so vainly,
    And sung with such faltering breath,
The Master, in infinite mercy,
    Offers the boon of death.

DAYBREAK

STEPHEN SPENDER
(1909–   )

At dawn she lay with her profile at that angle
Which, sleeping, seems the stone face of an
    angel;
Her hair a harp the hand of a breeze follows
To play, against the white cloud of the pillows.
Then in a flush of rose she woke, and her eyes
    were open
Swimming with blue through the rose flesh of
    dawn.
From her dew of lips, the drop of one word
Fell, from a dawn of fountains, when she
    murmured
"Darling," upon my heart the song of the first
    bird.
"My dream glides in my dream," she said,
    "come true.
I waken from you to my dream of you."
O then my waking dream dared to assume
The audacity of her sleep. Our dreams
Flowed into each other's arms, like streams.

I SAW MY DARLING ON
THE STREET . . .

FREDERICK MORGAN
(1922–   )

I saw my darling on the street
walking home with clothes in her arms—
clothes from the cleaners. She rippled along
past where the school was being built

on the next block. I called out to her—
shouting "Paula!" from my window.
Shouted twice, three times. A black
construction worker grinned at me

from the unfinished rooftop. Paula
paused—then turning, glanced behind her,
and at last—as I called her name once more—
looked up and smiled, and cried "I'm coming!"

Earlier that bright Autumn day
we had phoned the suburban hospital
where a old brave friend was slowly dying—
a loving voice, but faint and frail . . .

It all gives way to death in the end—
this shifting show of shapes that pass—
that much is clear, as time moves on
and pain outmatches early joy.

That's why I'm grateful for those times
when time itself comes to a stop
on some quite ordinary day,
comes to a stop for a random moment

in which the self gains breathing space
to renew itself outside of time—
as I'm renewed, who still hold fast
that pause made radiant by her smile.

EVENING HARMONY

CHARLES BAUDELAIRE
(1821–1867)

Now comes the hour when, in the quivering
    light,
Each flower to heaven exhales, a censer fair;
Perfumes and sounds wheel in the evening air,
A mournful waltz, a languorous, whirling
    flight!

Each flower to heaven exhales, a censer fair;
The violin sobs, a soul in sorrowing plight,
A mournful waltz, a languorous, whirling
    flight!
The sky, sad, lovely tomb, knows not of care.

The violin sobs, a soul in sorrowing plight,
A heart too tender for the void's dark lair.
The sky, sad, lovely tomb, knows not of care;
The sun sinks, drowned in his own blood, from
    sight.

A heart too tender for the void's dark lair
Gathers each memory of all past delight.
The sun sinks, drowned in his own blood, from
    sight;
And in my soul you shine, a monstrance rare!

TRANSLATED BY DOROTHY MARTIN

LAST NIGHT WITH RAFAELLA

DAVID ST. JOHN
(1949–   )

Last night, with Rafaella,

I sat at one of the outside tables
At *Rosati* watching the *ragazzi* on Vespas
Scream through the Piazza del Popolo

And talked again about changing my life,

Doing something meaningful—perhaps
Exploring a continent or discovering a vaccine,
Falling in love or over the white falls
Of a dramatic South American river!—
And Rafaella

Stroked the back of my wrist as I talked,

Smoothing the hairs until they lay as quietly
As wheat before the old authoritarian wind.

Rafaella had just returned from Milano
Where she'd supervised the Spring collection
Of a famous, even notorious, young designer—

A man whose name brought tears to the eyes
Of Contessas, movie stars, and diplomats' wives
Along the Via Condotti or the Rue
Du Faubourg-St. Honoré.

So I felt comfortable there, with Rafaella,
Discussing these many important things, I mean
The spiritual life, and my own
Long disenchantment with the ordinary world.

Comfortable because I knew she was a
    sophisticated,
Well-travelled woman, so impossible
To shock. A friend who'd
Often rub the opal on her finger so slowly

It made your mouth water,

The whole while telling you what it would be
    like
To feel her tongue addressing your ear.

And how could I not trust the advice
Of a woman who, with the ball of her
    exquisite thumb,
Carefully flared rouge along the white
    cheekbones
Of the most beautiful women in the world?

Last night, as we lay in the dark,
The windows of her bedroom open to the
    cypress,
To the stars, to the wind knocking at those stiff
Umbrella pines along her garden's edge,
I noticed as she turned slowly in the moonlight

A small tattoo just above her hip bone—

It was a dove in flight or an angel with its
Head tucked beneath its wing,

I couldn't tell in the shadows . . .

And as I kissed this new illumination of her
    body
Rafaella said, *Do you know how to tell a model?*
In fashion, they wear tattoos like singular beads
Along their hips,
                    but artists' models
Wear them like badges against the daily nakedness,
The way Celestine has above one nipple that
Minute yellow bee and above
The other an elaborate, cupped poppy . . .

I thought about this,
Pouring myself a little wine and listening
To the owls marking the distances, the
    geometries
Of the dark.
                    Rafaella's skin was
Slightly damp as I ran my fingertip
Along each delicate winged ridge of her
Collarbone, running the harp length of ribs
Before circling the shy angel . . .

And slowly, as the stars
Shifted in their rack of black complexities
    above,

Along my shoulder, Rafaella's hair fell in coils,

Like the frayed silk of some ancient tapestry,
Like the spun cocoons of the Orient—
Like a fragile ladder

To some whole other level of the breath.

THE BROKEN TOWER

HART CRANE
(1899–1932)

The bell-rope that gathers God at dawn
Dispatches me as though I dropped down the
  knell
Of a spent day—to wander the cathedral lawn
From pit to crucifix, feet chill on steps from
  hell.

Have you not heard, have you not seen that
  corps
Of shadows in the tower, whose shoulders sway
Antiphonal carillons launched before
The stars are caught and hived in the sun's ray?

The bells, I say, the bells break down their
    tower;
And swing I know not where. Their tongues
    engrave
Membrane through marrow, my long-scattered
    score
Of broken intervals. . . . And I, their sexton
    slave!

Oval encyclicals in canyons heaping
The impasse high with choir. Banked voices
    slain!
Pagodas, campaniles with reveilles outleaping—
O terraced echoes prostrate on the plain! . . .

And so it was I entered the broken world
To trace the visionary company of love, its
    voice
An instant in the wind (I know not whither
    hurled)
But not for long to hold each desperate choice.

My word I poured. But was it cognate, scored
Of that tribunal monarch of the air
Whose thigh embronzes earth, strikes crystal
    Word
In wounds pledged once to hope—cleft to
    despair?

The steep encroachments of my blood left me
No answer (could blood hold such a lofty tower
As flings the question true?)—or is it she
Whose sweet mortality stirs latent power?—

And through whose pulse I hear, counting the
        strokes
My veins recall and add, revived and sure
The angelus of wars my chest evokes:
What I hold healed, original now, and pure . . .

And builds, within, a tower that is not stone
(Not stone can jacket heaven)—but slip
Of pebbles—visible wings of silence sown
In azure circles, widening as they dip

The matrix of the heart, lift down the eye
That shrines the quiet lake and swells a
        tower . . .
The commodious, tall decorum of the sky
Unseals her earth, and lifts love in its shower.

THE BRIDGE OF SIGHS

STEVE ORLEN
(1942–   )

If you'll believe me when I tell you I have tried
To understand pleasure, the beginning of
  pleasure,
You'll know exactly how I watched my mother

That morning lounging in the red plush chair
In the gray, submerging shadows of the parlor
As she talked on the phone: that I stared

With each of my five years at the tender
Curve of her ankle as it moved down the high
  instep
Of her dry, clean, pale, and perfect foot and
  over

The toes, underneath to the arch. Oh, it just
  leapt!
It was the highest, most splendid arch,
More magnificent than the Arc de Triomphe in
  the newsreels

As the German soldiers marched beneath,
More delicate than the arches of the bridges
Of Venice, built by those gentlemen the Doges,

Paved by the feet of centuries of lovers
And saved from destruction by the American
  soldiers
On probably the same morning

I watched my mother's foot tense and relax,
And when she smiled down her long body at
  me,
And stroked my hair, and offered me the
  smooth beauty

Of her foot, and asked me, yes, to *rub it* just a
  little,
She said, right into the phone to whomever,
"Ahhh," the *ah* of the beginning of pleasure

That demands, even as it gives itself up,
That leaves you always ready to begin,
Always on the lip of things

Like a young harlot standing on the Bridge of
  Sighs
Waving goodbye to the soldiers of the losing
  side,
Waving hello to the soldiers of the winning
  side.

SHE WALKS IN BEAUTY

GEORGE GORDON, LORD BYRON
(1788–1824)

She walks in beauty, like the night
   Of cloudless climes and starry skies;
And all that's best of dark and bright
   Meet in her aspect and her eyes:
Thus mellowed to that tender light
   Which heaven to gaudy day denies.

One shade the more, one ray the less,
   Had half impaired the nameless grace
Which waves in every raven tress,
   Or softly lightens o'er her face;
Where thoughts serenely sweet express
   How pure, how dear their dwelling place.

And on that cheek, and o'er that brow,
   So soft, so calm, yet eloquent,
The smiles that win, the tints that glow,
   But tell of days in goodness spent,
A mind at peace with all below,
   A heart whose love is innocent!

GENGHIS CHAN: PRIVATE EYE

JOHN YAU
(1950–   )

I was floating through a cross section
with my dusty wineglass, when she entered,
a shivering bundle of shredded starlight.
You don't need words to tell a story,
a gesture will do. These days,
we're all parasites looking for a body
to cling to. I'm nothing more
than riffraff splendor drifting past the runway.
I always keep a supply of lamprey lipstick
    around,
just in case.
                    She laughed,
a slashed melody of small shrugs.
It had been raining in her left eye.
She began: a cloud or story
broken in two maybe four places,
wooden eyelids, and a scarf of human hair.
She paused: I offer you dervish bleakness
    and glistening sediment.
                            It was late
and we were getting jammed in deep.
I was on the other side, staring at
the snow covered moon pasted above the park.
A foul lump started making promises in my
    voice.

LOOKING INTO A FACE

Robert Bly
(1926–   )

Conversation brings us so close! Opening
The surfs of the body,
Bringing fish up near the sun,
And stiffening the backbones of the sea!

I have wandered in a face, for hours,
Passing through dark fires.
I have risen to a body
Not yet born,
Existing like a light around the body,
Through which the body moves like a sliding
    moon.

SUDDEN LIGHT

DANTE GABRIEL ROSSETTI
(1828–1882)

I have been here before,
    But when or how I cannot tell:
I know the grass beyond the door,
    The sweet keen smell,
The sighing sound, the lights around the shore.

You have been mine before,—
    How long ago I may not know:
But just when at that swallow's soar
    Your neck turned so,
Some veil did fall,—I knew it all of yore.

Has this been thus before?
    And shall not thus time's eddying flight
Still with our lives our love restore
    In death's despite,
And day and night yield one delight once more?

HOLDING THE THOUGHT OF LOVE

BERNADETTE MAYER
(1945–   )

And to render harmless a bomb or the like
Of such a pouring in different directions of love
Love scattered not concentrated love talked
    about,
So let's not talk of love the diffuseness of which
Round our heads (that oriole's song) like on the
    platforms
Of the subways and at their stations is today
    defused
As if by the scattering of light rays in a
    photograph
Of the softened reflection of a truck in a
    bakery window

You know I both understand what we found out
    and I don't
Hiking alone is too complex like a slap in the
    face
Of any joyous appointment even for the making
    of money

Abandoned to too large a crack in the unideal
    sphere of lack of summer
When it's winter, of wisdom in the
    astronomical arts, we as A & B
Separated then conjoin to see the sights of
    Avenue C

FROM *US*

ANNE SEXTON
(1928–1974)

I was wrapped in black
fur and white fur and
you undid me and then
you placed me in gold light
and then you crowned me,
while snow fell outside
the door in diagonal darts.
While a ten-inch snow
came down like stars
in small calcium fragments,
we were in our own bodies . . .
and you were in my body . . .
and at first I rubbed your
feet dry with a towel
because I was your slave
and then you called me princess.
Princess!

Oh then
I stood up in my gold skin
and I beat down the psalms
and I beat down the clothes
and you undid the bridle
and you undid the reins
and I undid the buttons,
the bones, the confusions,

the New England postcards,
the January ten o'clock night,

and we rose up like wheat,
acre after acre of gold,
and we harvested,
we harvested.

THE DALLIANCE OF THE EAGLES

WALT WHITMAN
(1819–1892)

Skirting the river road, (my forenoon walk, my
    rest,)
Skyward in air a sudden muffled sound, the
    dalliance of the eagles,
The rushing amorous contact high in space
    together,
The clinching interlocking claws, a living,
    fierce, gyrating wheel,
Four beating wings, two beaks, a swirling mass
    tight grappling,
In tumbling turning clustering loops, straight
    downward falling,
Till o'er the river pois'd, the twain yet one, a
    moment's lull,
A motionless still balance in the air, then
    parting, talons loosing,
Upward again on slow-firm pinions slanting,
    their separate diverse flights
She hers, he his, pursuing.

NEVER AGAIN WOULD BIRDS' SONG
BE THE SAME

ROBERT FROST
(1874–1963)

He would declare and could himself believe
That the birds there in all the garden round
From having heard the daylong voice of Eve
Had added to their own an oversound,
Her tone of meaning but without the words.
Admittedly an eloquence so soft
Could only have had an influence on birds
When call or laughter carried it aloft.
Be that as it may, she was in their song
Moreover her voice upon their voices crossed
Had now persisted in the woods so long
That probably it never would be lost.
Never again would birds' song be the same.
And to do that to birds was why she came.

FROM *I SING THE BODY ELECTRIC*

WALT WHITMAN

(1819–1892)

V

This is the female form,
A divine nimbus exhales from it from head to
    foot,
It attracts with fierce undeniable attraction,
I am drawn by its breath as if I were no more
    than a helpless vapor, all falls aside but
    myself and it,
Books, art, religion, time, the visible and solid
    earth, and what was expected of heaven or
    fear'd of hell, are now consumed,
Mad filaments, ungovernable shoots play out of
    it, the response likewise ungovernable,
Hair, bosom, hips, bend of legs, negligent
    falling hands all diffused, mine too
    diffused,
Ebb stung by the flow and flow stung by the
    ebb, love-flesh swelling and deliciously
    aching,
Limitless limpid jets of love hot and enormous,
    quivering jelly of love, white-blow and
    delirious juice,
Bridegroom night of love working surely and
    softly into the prostrate dawn,

Undulating into the willing and yielding day,
Lost in the cleave of the clasping and sweet-
flesh'd day.

This the nucleus—after the child is born of
woman, man is born of woman,
This the bath of birth, this the merge of small
and large, and the outlet again.

Be not ashamed women, your privilege encloses
the rest, and is the exit of the rest,
You are the gates of the body, and you are the
gates of the soul.

The female contains all qualities and tempers
them,
She is in her place and moves with perfect
balance,
She is all things duly veil'd, she is both passive
and active,
She is to conceive daughters as well as sons,
and sons as well as daughters.
As I see my soul reflected in Nature,
As I see through a mist, One with inexpressible
completeness, sanity, beauty,
As the bent head and arms folded over the
breast, the Female
I see.

These two poems might be seen as an argument between a reluctant beloved and a passionate lover. In response to Wordsworth's protestation that "the world is too much with us," a hundred years later Levertov argues for "plucking the fruit" of all that we, as sensual beings, are offered.

THE WORLD IS TOO MUCH WITH US

WILLIAM WORDSWORTH
(1770–1850)

The world is too much with us; late and soon,
Getting and spending, we lay waste our
    powers:
Little we see in Nature that is ours;
We have given our hearts away, a sordid boon!
This sea that bares her bosom to the moon;
The winds that will be howling at all hours,
And are up-gathered now like sleeping flowers;
For this, for everything, we are out of tune;
It moves us not.—Great God! I'd rather be
A Pagan suckled in a creed outworn;
So might I, standing on this pleasant lea,
Have glimpses that would make me less forlorn;
Have sight of Proteus rising from the sea;
Or hear old Triton blow his wreathèd horn.

O TASTE AND SEE

Denise Levertov
(1923–   )

The world is
not with us enough.
O taste and see

the subway Bible poster said,
meaning The Lord, meaning
if anything all that lives
to the imagination's tongue,

grief, mercy, language,
tangerine, weather, to
breathe them, bite,
savor, chew, swallow, transform

into our flesh our
deaths, crossing the street, plum, quince,
living in the orchard and being

hungry, and plucking
the fruit.

TO EARTHWARD

Robert Frost
(1874–1963)

Love at the lips was touch
As sweet as I could bear;
And once that seemed too much;
I lived on air

That crossed me from sweet things,
The flow of—was it musk
From hidden grapevine springs
Downhill at dusk?

I had the swirl and ache
From sprays of honeysuckle
That when they're gathered shake
Dew on the knuckle.

I craved strong sweets, but those
Seemed strong when I was young;
The petal of the rose
It was that stung.

Now no joy but lacks salt,
That is not dashed with pain
And weariness and fault;
I crave the stain

Of tears, the aftermark
Of almost too much love,
The sweet of bitter bark
And burning clove.

When stiff and sore and scarred
I take away my hand
From leaning on it hard
In grass and sand,

The hurt is not enough:
I long for weight and strength
To feel the earth as rough
To all my length.

TWO SONGS

ADRIENNE RICH
(1929–   )

1

Sex, as they harshly call it,
I fell into this morning
at ten o'clock, a drizzling hour
of traffic and wet newspapers.
I thought of him who yesterday
clearly didn't
turn me to a hot field
ready for plowing,
and longing for that young man
piercèd me to the roots
bathing every vein, etc.
All day he appears to me
touchingly desirable,
a prize one could wreck one's peace for.
I'd call it love if love
didn't take so many years
but lust too is a jewel
a sweet flower and what
pure happiness to know
all our high-toned questions
breed in a lively animal.

2

That "old last act"!
And yet sometimes
all seems post coitum triste
and I a mere bystander.
Somebody else is going off,
getting shot to the moon.
Or, a moon-race!
Split seconds after
my opposite number lands
I make it—
we lie fainting together
at a crater-edge
heavy as mercury in our moonsuits
till he speaks—
in a different language
yet one I've picked up
through cultural exchanges . . .
we murmur the first moonwords:
Spasibo. Thanks. O.K.

THE OLD CAUSES

Donald Revell
(1954–   )

My soul is wearied because of murderers.

Jeremiah 4:31

In the cool future, one will put off her dress by
     a window
and another will make the choice
between inhabiting and admiring.

We don't live long enough, any of us, to outlast
     history.
We shall not love with our bodies again
except in the coronal streets of paintings,

the unjust happiness and lamplight of the ratty
     voyeur
for ones so terribly thin now
without the little flags of their clothes.

Great tyrants understood the flesh and our
     nostalgia for it.
The glory of the rainy square
alive with atoms of loud speech
The glory of oblique pillars
of sunlight on the tousled hairs of a bed
The glory of not taking you in my arms now
but letting the paradise of the next day
waken to find you already there

teaching me to live with no purpose
and the endless rain on the public square better
    than heaven.

I dream of the deprived utopias that may yet
    arrive.
I see myself repeating a kind of courtship.
There is a messy apartment
brightened here and there by the subjective
    icons
of a woman's life before I knew her.
Somehow, I translate all of that
into the struggle and final triumph
of all of the people shouting one name,
not my name, but one I know intimately,
and then it is my right to go to bed with her.

In the cool future, the apartments and unfeeling
    icons
will face each other across our bodies.
We shall count for very little

or maybe I shall have learned to make the right
    choice, tendering
the little flags of her clothes
between my hands like a birthplace

or like the silhouette of my mother by the
    broken glass
of the apartment she died in
crowned with the future's coronal of lamplight.

TO HIS COY MISTRESS

ANDREW MARVELL
(1621–1678)

Had we but world enough, and time,
This coyness, lady, were no crime.
We would sit down, and think which way
To walk, and pass our long love's day.
Thou by the Indian Ganges' side
Shouldst rubies find: I by the tide
Of Humber would complain. I would
Love you ten years before the flood,
And you should, if you please, refuse
Till the conversion of the Jews;
My vegetable love should grow
Vaster than empires and more slow;
An hundred years should go to praise
Thine eyes, and on thy forehead gaze;
Two hundred to adore each breast,
But thirty thousand to the rest;
An age at least to every part,
And the last age should show your heart.
For, lady, you deserve this state,
Nor would I love at lower rate.

But at my back I always hear
Time's wingèd chariot hurrying near,
And yonder all before us lie
Deserts of vast eternity.
Thy beauty shall no more be found,
Nor, in thy marble vault, shall sound
My echoing song; then worms shall try
That long-preserved virginity,
And your quaint honor turn to dust,
And into ashes all my lust:
The grave's a fine and private place,
But none, I think, do there embrace.
    Now, therefore, while the youthful hue
Sits on thy skin like morning dew,
And while thy willing soul transpires
At every pore with instant fires,
Now let us sport us while we may,
And now, like amorous birds of prey,
Rather at once our time devour,
Than languish in his slow-chapped power.
Let us roll all our strength and all
Our sweetness up into one ball,
And tear our pleasures with rough strife
Thorough the iron gates of life;
Thus, though we cannot make our sun
Stand still, yet we will make him run.

CASHEL OF MUNSTER

(From the Irish)

SAMUEL FERGUSON
(1810–1886)

I'd wed you without herds, without money, or
    rich array,
And I'd wed you on a dewy morning at day-
    dawn grey;
My bitter woe it is, love, that we are not far
    away
In Cashel town, though the bare deal board
    were our marriage bed this day!

Oh, fair maid, remember the green hillside,
Remember how I hunted about the valleys
    wide;
Time now has worn me; my locks are turned to
    grey,
The year is scarce and I am poor, but send me
    not, love, away!

Oh, deem not my blood is of base strain, my
    girl,
Oh, deem not my birth was as the birth of the
    churl;
Marry me, and prove me, and say soon you
    will,
That noble blood is written on my right side
    still!

My purse holds no red gold, no coin of the
    silver white,
No herds are mine to drive through the long
    twilight!
But the pretty girl that would take me, all bare
    though I be and lone,
Oh, I'd take her with me kindly to the county
    Tyrone.

Oh, my girl, I can see 'tis in trouble you are,
And oh, my girl, I see 'tis your people's
    reproach you bear:
'I am a girl in trouble for his sake with whom I
    fly,
And, oh, may no other maiden know such
    reproach as I!'

WILL YOU PERHAPS
CONSENT TO BE

Delmore Schwartz
(1913–1966)

Will you perhaps consent to be
Now that a little while is still
(Ruth of sweet wind) now that a little while
My mind's continuing and unreleasing wind
Touches this single of your flowers, this one
    only,
Will you perhaps consent to be
My many-branched, small and dearest tree?

My mind's continuing and unreleasing wind
—The wind which is wild and restless, tired
    and asleep,
The wind which is tired, wild and still
    continuing,
The wind which is chill, and warm, wet, soft,
    in every influence,
Lusts for Paris, Crete and Pergamus,
Is suddenly off for Paris and Chicago,
Judaea, San Francisco, the Midi
—May I perhaps return to you
Wet with an Attic dust and chill from Norway
My dear, so-many-branched smallest tree?

Would you perhaps consent to be
The very rack and crucifix of winter, winter's
    wild
Knife-edged, continuing and unreleasing,
Intent and stripping, ice-caressing wind?
My dear, most dear, so-many-branched tree,
My mind's continuing and unreleasing wind
Touches this single of your flowers, faith in me,
Wide as the—sky!—accepting as the (air)!
—Consent, consent, consent to be
My many-branched, small and dearest tree.

WINTER POEM

FREDERICK MORGAN
(1922–   )

We made love on a winter afternoon
and when we woke, hours had turned and
   changed,
the moon was shining, and the earth was new.
The city, with its lines and squares, was gone:
our room had placed itself on a small hill
surrounded by dark woods frosted in snow
and meadows where the flawless drifts lay
   deep.
No men there—some small animals all fur
stared gently at us with soft-shining eyes
as we stared back through the chill frosty
   panes.
Absolute cold gave us our warmth that night,
we held hands in the pure throes of delight,
the air we breathed was washed clean by the
   snow.

ACKNOWLEDGMENTS

"The Ache of Marriage" by Denise Levertov from *Poems 1960–1967*. Copyright © 1964 by Denise Levertov Goodman. Reprinted by permission of New Directions Publishing Corporation.

"Age to Youth" by Judith Wright from *Collected Poems*, © Judith Wright, 1971. Reprinted by permission of Collins/Angus & Robertson Publishers.

"Anniversary" from *Poems* by Richmond Lattimore. Copyright © 1957 by University of Michigan Press, renewed 1972 by Richmond Lattimore. Reprinted by permission of the publisher.

"As a Possible Lover" from *The Dead Lecturer* reprinted by permission of Sterling Lord Literistic, Inc. Copyright © 1964 by Amiri Baraka.

"At Baia" by H.D. from *Collected Poems 1912–1944*. Copyright © 1982 by the Estate of Hilda Doolittle. Reprinted by permission of New Directions Publishing Corporation.

"Blue Girls" from *Selected Poems*, third edition, revised and enlarged, by John Crowe Ransom. Copyright 1924, 1927 by Alfred A. Knopf, Inc. and renewed 1952, 1955 by John Crowe Ransom. Reprinted by permission of Alfred A. Knopf, Inc.

"The Bridge of Sighs" by Steve Orlen appeared originally in *The Atlantic Monthly* and then in *The Best American Poetry 1989*, Donald Hall, ed. Reprinted by permission of Steve Orlen.

"A Broken Appointment" from *The Complete Poems of Thomas Hardy*, edited by James Gibson (New York: Macmillan, 1978).

"The Broken Tower" reprinted from *The Complete Poems and Selected Letters and Prose of Hart Crane*, Edited by Brom Weber, by permission of Liveright Publishing Corporation. Copyright 1933, © 1958, 1966 by Liveright Publishing Corporation.

"The Columbine" by Jones Very from *Essays and Poems* (Little, Brown & Co., 1839).

"The Dalliance of the Eagles" from The Comprehensive Reader's Edition of *Leaves of Grass* by Walt Whitman, ed. by Harold W. Blodgett and Sculley Bradley. Reprinted by permission of NYU Press.

"Daybreak" from *Collected Poems 1928–1953* by Stephen Spender. Copyright 1942 and renewed 1970 by Stephen Spender. Reprinted by permission of Random House, Inc.

"Distracted" by Pedro Salinas from *Love Poems from Spain and Spanish America*. English translation copyright © 1986 by Perry Higman. Reprinted by permission of City Lights Books.

"Evening Harmony" by Charles Baudelaire from *Flowers of Evil*. Copyright © 1955, 1962 by New Directions Publishing Corporation. Reprinted by permission of New Directions Publishing Corporation.

"First Love" from *The Poems of John Clare*, ed. by Tibble and Tibble. Reprinted by permission of J. M. Dent & Sons Ltd.

"Genghis Chan: Private Eye" by John Yau from *Sulfur* #19, 1987. Reprinted by permission of the magazine.

"Green, Green, and Green Again . . ." from *Collected Poems* by Conrad Aiken. Copyright © 1953, 1970 by Conrad Aiken; renewed 1981 by Mary Aiken. Reprinted by permission of Oxford University Press, Inc.

"Holding the Thought of Love" by Bernadette Mayer from *Exquisite Corpse*, vol. 5, no. 9–12, 1987. Reprinted by permission of the magazine.

136

INDEX OF TITLES

INDEX OF AUTHORS AND TRANSLATORS